Please make sure to read the enclosed Ninja Owner's Guide prior to using your unit.

NINJA® STORM™

Blend Easy, Chop Happy: 75 Simple Recipes
Smoothies, Quick Meals, and Entertaining

Master Prep and Ninja are registered trademarks of SharkNinja Operating LLC.
STORM is a trademark of SharkNinja Operating LLC.

Editors and Content: Bob Warden, Katie Barry, Elizabeth Skladany, and Daniel Davis

Recipe Development: SharkNinja Culinary Innovation Team and Great Flavors Recipe Development Team

Design/Layout: Liz Parmalee and Leslie Anne Feagley

Creative/Photo Director: Lauren Wiernasz

Photography: Quentin Bacon and Gary Sloan

Published in the United States of America by

Partners-In-Publishing LLC
P.O. Box 250
New Hope, PA 19838

QB751Q ISBN: 978-1-4951-8605-9

10   9   8   7   6   5   4   3   2   1

Printed in China

Table of Contents

Get ready to take meal prep by storm.

Congratulations on the purchase of your new Ninja® Storm™. With all the easy-to-make recipes in this book, we've got a feeling you'll be dishing out delicious smoothies, dips, drinks, and salads left and right.

That's because your Ninja® Storm™ features a compact power pod and a 40-ounce Master Prep® Bowl, which doubles as a blender and a food processor, giving you the power and functionality of two kitchen appliances in one simple system.

With all that blend-and-chop convenience, you'll find it's easier than ever to fit good-for-you dishes into your everyday routine and restaurant-quality frozen blended cocktails into your next get-together. Yep, the Ninja Storm will take you from smoothies and rich dips to fresh chopped salads and wholesome meals in just a few pulses.

Notice: Remove the Master Pod, Splashguard, and 4-Blade Assembly after processing.
Some ingredients have the potential to expand after processing.

Pulsing makes perfect.

The key to perfectly blended and chopped ingredients is all in your hands. Literally. When you're working with heavier ingredients or need smoother results, press down in 2-second pulses. When using lighter ingredients for salsas, dips, or chopped salads, use shorter, half-second pulses.

Feel-good meal swaps.

With a few simple tweaks, you can change up your favorite recipes without losing out on flavor.

	INSTEAD OF	SUBSTITUTE WITH THIS
DAIRY	Sour cream, full fat	Plain lowfat yogurt, plain Greek yogurt
	Milk, evaporated	Evaporated skim milk
	Whole milk	1% milk, nonfat milk, almond milk
	Cheddar cheese	Lowfat cheddar cheese
	Ice cream	Frozen yogurt or sorbet
	Cream cheese	Neufchâtel or light cream cheese
	Whipped cream	Light whipped topping
	Ricotta cheese	Lowfat ricotta cheese
	Cream	Fat-free half & half, evaporated skim milk
	Yogurt, fruit flavored	Plain yogurt with fresh fruit slices
PROTEIN	Bacon	Canadian bacon, turkey bacon, smoked turkey, or lean prosciutto (Italian ham)
	Ground beef	Extra-lean or lean ground beef, ground chicken or turkey breast, tofu, tempeh
	Meats as the main ingredient	Three times as many vegetables as the meat on pizzas or in casseroles, soups, and stews
	Eggs	Two egg whites or $1/4$ cup egg substitute for each whole egg
OTHER	Soups, creamed	Nonfat-milk-based soups, puréed carrots, potatoes, or tofu for thickening agents
	Soups, sauces, dressings, crackers; or canned meats	Low-sodium or no-sodium versions

	INSTEAD OF	SUBSTITUTE WITH THIS
GRAINS	Bread, white	Whole-grain bread
	Breadcrumbs, dry	Crushed bran cereal or almond meal
	Pasta, enriched (white)	Whole wheat pasta
	Rice, white	Brown rice, wild rice, bulgur, or pearl barley
FAT	Butter, margarine, shortening, or oil in baked goods	Applesauce or prune purée for half of the called-for butter, shortening, or oil; butter spreads or shortenings specially formulated for baking that don't have trans fats (Note: To avoid dense, soggy, or flat baked goods, don't substitute oil for butter or shortening. Also, don't substitute diet, whipped, or tub-style margarine for regular margarine.)
	Butter, margarine, shortening, or oil to prevent sticking	Cooking spray or nonstick pans
	Mayonnaise	Reduced-calorie mayonnaise-type salad dressing or reduced-calorie, reduced-fat mayonnaise
	Oil-based marinades	Wine, balsamic vinegar, fruit juice, or fat-free broth
SUGAR	Sugar	In most baked goods you can reduce the amount of sugar by half; intensify sweetness by adding vanilla, nutmeg, or cinnamon.
	Syrup	Puréed fruit, such as applesauce, or low-calorie, sugar-free syrup
	Chocolate chips	Dried cranberries
SAUCES	Soy sauce	Low-sodium soy sauce, tamari sauce (which is gluten-free), hot mustard
SALT	Salt	Herbs, spices, citrus juices (lemon, lime, orange), rice vinegar, salt-free seasoning mixes or herb blends, low-sodium soy sauce (cuts the sodium in half by equal volume while boosting flavor)
	Seasoning salt, such as garlic salt, celery salt, or onion salt	Herb-only seasonings, such as garlic powder, celery seed, or onion flakes. Finely chopped herbs, garlic, celery, or onions.

Crowd-pleasing made easy.

With the power of two appliances in one, your Ninja® Storm™ is as great for entertaining as it is for making everyday meals. But we know menu planning can be intimidating, so we've lined up some thought-starters for you. All of these themed recipes can be found right in this cookbook—armed with your Ninja® Storm™, you're the host with the most in a few pulses flat.

Mexican Brunch
Frozen Margarita (page 81)
Best Blender Salsa (page 72)
Midwest Breakfast Burrito (page 40)

Casual Ladies Night
Frozen Sangria (page 83)
Tandoori Turkey Pita (page 67)
Cucumber Feta Dip (page 79)

Classic Brunch
Classic Bloody Mary (page 75)
Spinach Feta Strata (page 36)
Chicken Apple Sausage (page 29)

Comfort Classics
Spinach Artichoke Dip (page 74)
Tomato Basil Soup (page 66)
Lemon Bars (page 98)

Afternoon Picnic
Watermelon Quench (page 12)
Curry Chicken Salad (page 68)
Classic Hummus (page 76)

Tropical Summer Cookout
Piña Colada (page 84)
Salmon Burgers (page 69)
Mango Rum Remoulade (page 49)

Spicy Pineapple Recharge
page 10

PREP TIME: **5 minutes**   MAKES: **4 servings**
CONTAINER: 40-ounce Master Prep® Bowl

Spicy Pineapple Recharge

Ingredients

3 cups fresh pineapple chunks

½-inch piece fresh ginger, peeled

2 limes, peeled, cut in half

1 small jalapeño pepper,
seeds removed

1 ½ cups orange juice

1 cup ice

Directions

1 Place all ingredients into the 40-ounce Master Prep Bowl in the order listed.

2 PULSE until smooth, using long pulses.

 RIPE PINEAPPLES WILL IMPART THE PERFECT AMOUNT OF SWEETNESS TO BLEND WITH THE HINT OF HEAT AND FRAGRANT TASTE OF GINGER.

Lean Green Ninja

Ingredients

1 1/2 small ripe bananas

3/4 cup kale leaves

3/4 cup baby spinach

1 1/2 cups fresh pineapple chunks

1 1/2 cups fresh mango chunks

1 1/2 cups ice

1 1/2 cups coconut water

Directions

1 Place all ingredients into the 40-ounce Master Prep Bowl in the order listed.

2 PULSE until smooth, using long pulses.

PREP TIME: **5 minutes**   MAKES: **4 servings**
CONTAINER: **40-ounce Master Prep® Bowl**

Watermelon Quench

Ingredients

2 ½ cups fresh watermelon chunks

2 cups pomegranate juice

1 cup frozen peach slices

Directions

1 Place all ingredients into the 40-ounce Master Prep Bowl in the order listed.

2 PULSE until smooth, using long pulses.

PREP TIME: **5 minutes**   MAKES: **4 servings**
CONTAINER: **40-ounce Master Prep® Bowl**

Peach Soother Smoothie

Ingredients

2 teaspoons fresh ginger, peeled

1 $1/2$ pears, cored, chopped

2 tablespoons ground flaxseed

1 $1/2$ cups plain nonfat kefir

$3/4$ cup nonfat yogurt

1 $1/4$ cups frozen peaches

Directions

1 Place all ingredients into the 40-ounce Master Prep Bowl in the order listed.

2 PULSE until smooth, using long pulses.

PREP TIME: **5 minutes**   MAKES: **2 servings**
CONTAINER: *40-ounce Master Prep® Bowl*

Pear & Green Tea Smoothie

Ingredients

1 pear, cored, cut in quarters

1 cup spinach

1 lemon, peeled, cut in quarters

1 tablespoon honey

2 cups chilled brewed green tea

1 1/2 cups ice

Directions

1 Place all ingredients into the 40-ounce Master Prep Bowl in the order listed.

2 PULSE until smooth, using long pulses.

PREP TIME: **5 minutes**   MAKES: **4 servings**
CONTAINER: **40-ounce Master Prep® Bowl**

Tropical Squeeze Smoothie

Ingredients

1 small ripe banana

1 orange, peeled, cut in quarters

$1/2$ cup fresh pineapple chunks

2 cups water

1 cup nonfat yogurt

1 $1/4$ cups frozen mango chunks

Directions

1 Place all ingredients into the 40-ounce Master Prep Bowl in the order listed.

2 PULSE until smooth, using long pulses.

PREP TIME: **5 minutes**   MAKES: **2 servings**
CONTAINER: **40-ounce Master Prep® Bowl**

Apple Berry Protein

Ingredients

1 cup red seedless grapes

$^1/_2$ apple, cored, chopped

2 tablespoons vanilla protein powder

$^3/_4$ cup coconut water

1 $^1/_4$ cups frozen blueberries

Directions

1 Place all ingredients into the 40-ounce Master Prep Bowl in the order listed.

2 PULSE until smooth, using long pulses.

PREP TIME: **5 minutes**   MAKES: **4 servings**

CONTAINER: **40-ounce Master Prep® Bowl**

Cool Honeydew Cucumber

Ingredients

$1/2$ cucumber, peeled,
cut in 1-inch chunks

1 cup fresh honeydew melon
chunks

$1 1/2$ cups fresh pineapple chunks

1 cup water

1 cup ice

Directions

1 Place all ingredients into the 40-ounce Master Prep Bowl in the order listed.

2 PULSE until smooth, using long pulses.

PREP TIME: **5 minutes**   MAKES: **4 servings**
CONTAINER: **40-ounce Master Prep® Bowl**

Strawberry Banana Protein Smoothie

Ingredients

1 ½ cups frozen strawberries

2 small ripe bananas

¾ cup nonfat Greek yogurt

1 ½ cups orange juice

1 scoop vanilla protein powder

Directions

1 Place all ingredients into the 40-ounce Master Prep Bowl in the order listed.

2 PULSE until smooth, using long pulses.

 BE CREATIVE AND FEEL FREE TO SUBSTITUTE YOUR FAVORITE FROZEN FRUIT, USING BLUEBERRIES, RASPBERRIES, PINEAPPLE OR MANGO.

PREP TIME: 5 minutes   MAKES: 4 servings
CONTAINER: 40-ounce Master Prep® Bowl

Easy Does It Green Juice

Ingredients

$^1/_3$ cucumber, peeled,
cut in quarters

1 cup green seedless grapes

1 cup baby spinach

$^1/_2$ pear, cut in half, cored

$^1/_2$ small ripe banana

$^3/_4$ cup coconut water

1 cup ice

Directions

1 Place all ingredients into the 40-ounce Master Prep Bowl in the order listed.

2 PULSE until smooth, using long pulses.

Power Ball

Ingredients

2 ¼ cups frozen blueberries

2 ¾ cups unsweetened light coconut milk

1 ½ small ripe bananas

2 teaspoons unsweetened cocoa powder

Directions

1 Place all ingredients into the 40-ounce Master Prep Bowl in the order listed.

2 PULSE until smooth, using long pulses.

PREP TIME: **5 minutes**   MAKES: **4 servings**
CONTAINER: **40-ounce Master Prep® Bowl**

Island Mood Boost

Ingredients

1 1/2 cups fresh pineapple chunks

1 1/2 small ripe bananas

1 1/2 cups frozen strawberries

1 1/2 cups frozen mango chunks

3 cups coconut water

Directions

1 Place all ingredients into the 40-ounce Master Prep Bowl in the order listed.

2 PULSE until smooth, using long pulses.

PREP TIME: 5 minutes   MAKES: 4 servings
CONTAINER: 40-ounce Master Prep® Bowl

Fruit Salad Smoothie

Ingredients

$^1/_2$ cup frozen pineapple chunks

$^3/_4$ cup frozen mango chunks

1 cup green seedless grapes

1 small ripe banana, cut in half

$^1/_2$ apple, peeled, cored,
cut in half

1 cup orange juice

Directions

1 Place all ingredients into the 40-ounce Master Prep Bowl in the order listed.

2 PULSE until smooth, using long pulses.

PREP TIME: 5 minutes   MAKES: 4 servings
CONTAINER: 40-ounce Master Prep® Bowl

Chai-Spiced Eye Opener

Ingredients

2 cups baby spinach

2 ripe pears, cored, cut in quarters

2 cups chilled brewed chai tea

1 cup frozen mango chunks

1/2-inch piece fresh ginger, peeled

1 tablespoon plus 1 teaspoon fresh lemon juice

Dash salt

Directions

1 Place all ingredients into the 40-ounce Master Prep Bowl in the order listed.

2 PULSE until smooth, using long pulses.

PREP TIME: 15 minutes   COOK TIME: 10–12 minutes   MAKES: 8 servings
CONTAINER: 40-ounce Master Prep® Bowl

Chicken Apple Sausage

Ingredients

1 small onion, cut in quarters

2 apples, peeled, cored,
cut in quarters

1/3 cup fresh sage leaves

1 tablespoon olive oil

1 pound boneless skinless chicken
thighs, cut in 2-inch cubes

Pinch cinnamon

3/4 teaspoon salt

3/4 teaspoon ground black pepper

Directions

1 Preheat oven to 350°F. Line a cookie sheet with parchment paper; set aside. Place the onion, apples, and sage into the 40-ounce Master Prep Bowl. PULSE 5 to 7 times, using short pulses, until finely chopped.

2 Heat the olive oil in a medium skillet over medium heat. Add apple mixture and cook, sautéing until aromatic and tender. Remove from heat and place in a large bowl to cool.

3 Place cubed chicken into the 40-ounce Master Prep Bowl and PULSE, using long pulses, until finely ground, about 10 times. Add the ground chicken to the bowl with the apple mixture. Add the cinnamon, salt, and pepper. Mix well, using your hands.

4 Form mixture into eight patties and place on prepared cookie sheet. Bake 10 to 12 minutes, until cooked through.

DO NOT BLEND HOT INGREDIENTS.

PREP TIME: **10** minutes COOK TIME: **15** minutes MAKES: **16** (1-ounce) pancakes (4–6 servings)
CONTAINER: 40-ounce Master Prep Bowl

Lemon Ricotta Pancakes

Ingredients

1 cup pancake mix

$1/4$ teaspoon ground ginger

$1/2$ teaspoon cinnamon

1 large egg

$3/4$ cup lowfat buttermilk

1 $1/2$ tablespoons melted butter

$1/2$ cup ricotta cheese

$1/2$ teaspoon lemon zest

1 tablespoon canola oil

Directions

1 In a small bowl, combine pancake mix, ginger, and cinnamon.

2 Place egg, buttermilk, melted butter, ricotta cheese, lemon zest, and dry mixture into the 40-ounce Master Prep Bowl. PULSE to combine, using long pulses.

3 Heat a large nonstick skillet with 1 tablespoon canola oil over medium heat. Spoon 2 to 3 tablespoons of batter onto skillet at a time. Cook until pancakes start to bubble, about 1 to 2 minutes.

4 Flip with a spatula, and cook until underside is browned, about 1 to 2 minutes. Transfer to a platter, and serve with your favorite topping.

PREP TIME: **15 minutes**   COOK TIME: **12–14 minutes**   MAKES: **8 scones**
CONTAINER: **40-ounce Master Prep Bowl**

Date & Orange Scones

Ingredients

1 3/4 cups all-purpose flour

2 tablespoons baking powder

2 tablespoons olive oil

1 tablespoon agave nectar

3/4 cup dates,
pits removed, chopped

3/4 cup orange juice

2 tablespoons orange zest

1 teaspoon ground cinnamon

1/2 teaspoon ground ginger

Directions

1 Preheat oven to 375°F. Position rack in middle of oven.

2 Place flour, baking powder, oil, and agave nectar into the 40-ounce Master Prep Bowl. PULSE 5 times, until all ingredients are combined and dough forms coarse crumbs.

3 Add dates, orange juice, orange zest, cinnamon, and ginger. PULSE until combined completely.

4 Shape dough into triangles, and place on a greased baking pan, 1 1/2 inches apart. Bake 12 to 14 minutes until light golden brown.

PREP TIME: **20** minutes   CHILL TIME: **1** hour   MAKES: **12** bars
CONTAINER: **40-ounce Master Prep Bowl**

Superfood Snack Bars

Ingredients

1 cup raw almonds

8 dates, pits removed

¼ cup dried cherries

2 tablespoons unsweetened coconut flakes

1 tablespoon hemp seed

2 teaspoons maple syrup

2 tablespoons toasted pumpkin seeds

1 tablespoon water

Directions

1 Line an 8x8-inch baking dish with plastic wrap; set aside.

2 Place all ingredients, except the pumpkin seeds and water, into the 40-ounce Master Prep Bowl in the order listed.

3 PULSE until dates have been broken down and mixture is coarsely chopped. Scrape down sides of the bowl as necessary.

4 Add pumpkin seeds and water to the 40-ounce Master Prep Bowl and PULSE until ingredients are fully combined.

5 Press mixture firmly into the lined baking dish, cover, and refrigerate at least 1 hour.

6 Invert onto a cutting board, remove plastic, and cut into 2-inch square bars. Wrap pieces in plastic wrap to store.

PREP TIME: **5 minutes**   COOK TIME: **5 minutes**   MAKES: **2 servings**
CONTAINER: **40-ounce Master Prep® Bowl**

Tomato Herb Omelet

Ingredients

4 eggs

1 tablespoon fresh parsley leaves

1 tablespoon fresh dill

$1/4$ cup fresh spinach

1 green onion, cut in 3 pieces

$1/8$ teaspoon salt

$1/8$ teaspoon ground black pepper

Vegetable cooking spray

$1/2$ cup shredded cheddar cheese

4 slices vine-ripened tomato

Directions

1 Place all ingredients except cooking spray, cheese, and tomato into the 40-ounce Master Prep Bowl in the order listed.

2 PULSE, using short pulses, until herbs are finely chopped.

3 Lightly spray a nonstick pan with cooking spray and place over medium-high heat. Add half the egg mixture and, using a rubber spatula, gently push the cooked edges of the eggs into the center of the pan, allowing the raw eggs to reach the edges and cook. When the eggs are cooked through, sprinkle half the cheese and two tomato slices on one half of the eggs, then fold over to form an omelet.

4 Repeat with remaining egg mixture, cheese, and tomato slices to make a second omelet.

Fresh Veggie Frittata

Ingredients

Vegetable cooking spray

1 stalk broccoli, cut in 2-inch florets

$1/2$ red bell pepper, seeds removed, cut in half

$1/4$ onion, peeled

1 clove garlic

1 tablespoon olive oil

6 eggs

$3/4$ cup grated Parmesan cheese, divided

$1/2$ teaspoon dried basil

$1/2$ teaspoon salt

$1/8$ teaspoon ground black pepper

Directions

1 Preheat oven to 350°F. Spray a 9x9-inch square baking dish with cooking spray; set aside. Place broccoli, red pepper, onion and garlic into the 40-ounce Master Prep Bowl. PULSE, using short pulses, until roughly chopped.

2 In a medium skillet over medium-high heat, heat olive oil. Add chopped vegetables and cook until softened, about 10 minutes. Transfer to prepared baking dish.

3 Add the eggs, $1/2$ cup Parmesan, basil, salt and pepper. Blend for 15 to 20 seconds, until smooth. Pour egg mixture over vegetables and sprinkle remaining cheese on top. Bake for 20 to 22 minutes or until center is set and top is lightly browned.

PREP TIME: 15 minutes plus 4 hours rest   COOK TIME: 25 minutes   MAKES: 8 servings
CONTAINER: 40-ounce Master Prep® Bowl

Spinach Feta Strata

Ingredients

Cooking spray

1 loaf day-old French bread, torn into bite-sized pieces

5 large eggs

1 cup half & half

1/2 cup cubed Monterey Jack cheese

1/2 cup cubed feta cheese

1 cup frozen spinach, thawed, squeezed of excess liquid

1/2 teaspoon salt

1/4 teaspoon ground nutmeg

1/4 teaspoon ground black pepper

Directions

1 Coat a round 9-inch baking pan with cooking spray and place the torn bread into the pan. Set aside.

2 Add the remaining ingredients to the 40-ounce Master Prep Bowl in the order listed.

3 PULSE, using long pulses, until mixed well. Pour the mixture over the bread then cover and chill for 4 hours to allow egg mixture to soak into the bread.

4 Preheat oven to 350°F. Bake for 20 to 25 minutes until puffed up and golden brown. Serve hot.

PREP TIME: **15 minutes**   COOK TIME: **20 minutes**   MAKES: **4 servings**
CONTAINER: **40-ounce Master Prep® Bowl**

Turkey Hash

Ingredients

¹/₂ medium onion, peeled,
cut in half

¹/₂ red bell pepper, seeds removed,
cut in half

1 clove garlic

1 pound uncooked turkey breast,
cut in 2-inch cubes

1 tablespoon vegetable oil

1 pound sweet potato, peeled, cut
in 1-inch cubes, cooked

³/₄ cup low-sodium chicken broth

1 teaspoon dried thyme

³/₄ teaspoon salt

³/₄ teaspoon ground black pepper

Directions

1 Place the onion, red pepper, and garlic into the 40-ounce Master Prep Bowl and PULSE, using short pulses, to desired chop. Remove vegetables and set aside.

2 Place the cubed turkey into the 40-ounce Master Prep Bowl and PULSE, using long pulses, until finely chopped.

3 Heat the oil in a medium skillet over medium heat. Add vegetable mixture, and sauté until tender, about 4 minutes.

4 Add the ground turkey and cook for 4 minutes, then add the remaining ingredients and cook for 10 minutes or until turkey is cooked through, stirring occasionally.

PREP TIME: **5 minutes**   REST TIME: **1 hour**   COOK TIME: **5 minutes**   MAKES: **8 servings**

CONTAINER: **40-ounce Master Prep® Bowl**

Buckwheat Boosted Pancakes

Ingredients

2 cups lowfat buttermilk

2 eggs

⅓ cup canola oil

1 cup buckwheat flour

1 cup all-purpose flour

2 teaspoons baking soda

2 teaspoons sugar

1 teaspoon salt

2 tablespoons honey

Directions

1 Place all ingredients into the 40-ounce Master Prep Bowl in the order listed.

2 PULSE 3 times, using short pulses, and then blend for 30 seconds until smooth. Chill batter for 1 hour before using.

3 Lightly spray a skillet with vegetable cooking spray and place over medium heat. Pour pancake batter in desired size and cook until small bubbles form. Flip and continue cooking until center is puffed and springs back when gently pushed.

PREP TIME: **10 minutes**   COOK TIME: **5 minutes**   MAKES: **6 servings**
CONTAINER: **40-ounce Master Prep® Bowl**

Midwest Breakfast Burrito

Ingredients

4 ounces cooked ham, cut in
2-inch cubes

$1/2$ medium green bell pepper,
cut in half

$1/2$ cup cubed lowfat cheddar
cheese

$1/8$ yellow onion

9 large eggs

$1/4$ teaspoon salt

$1/2$ teaspoon ground black pepper

6 (6-inch) whole wheat flour
tortillas

1 $1/4$ cups Best Blender
Salsa, page 72

Directions

1 Place all ingredients, except flour tortillas and salsa, into the 40-ounce Master Prep Bowl in the order listed.

2 PULSE, using short pulses, until finely chopped.

3 Lightly spray a skillet with vegetable cooking spray and place on medium-high heat. Add the egg mixture and stir until eggs are cooked through.

4 Divide the mixture onto each tortilla and top with Best Blender Salsa. Roll up each tortilla and serve.

Banana & Oats

Ingredients

1 small ripe banana

1 tablespoon shelled walnuts

1 cup lowfat milk

½ cup cold, cooked oatmeal

¼ teaspoon ground cinnamon

½ cup nonfat vanilla yogurt

Directions

1 Place all ingredients into the 40-ounce Master Prep Bowl in the order listed.

2 PULSE until smooth, using long pulses.

 NINJA KNOW-HOW CHANGE IT UP WITH FRESH BERRIES INSTEAD OF THE BANANA.

PREP TIME: 5 minutes   MAKES: 2 servings
CONTAINER: 40-ounce Master Prep® Bowl

Mocha Banana Shake

Ingredients

2 small frozen ripe bananas

1/2 cup chilled, brewed coffee

3 tablespoons creamy almond butter

2 teaspoons unsweetened cocoa powder

2 teaspoons agave nectar

1 cup unsweetened almond milk

Dash sea salt

Directions

1 Place all ingredients into the 40-ounce Master Prep Bowl in the order listed.

2 PULSE until smooth, using long pulses.

PREP TIME: 5 minutes   MAKES: 4 servings
CONTAINER: 40-ounce Master Prep® Bowl

Autumn Balancer

Ingredients

1 1/2 cups cooked sweet potato

2 cups unsweetened almond milk

1/4 cup maple syrup

2 teaspoons ground flaxseed

1/2 teaspoon ground turmeric

1 teaspoon salt

1 1/2 cups ice

Directions

1 Place all ingredients into the 40-ounce Master Prep Bowl in the order listed.

2 PULSE until smooth, using long pulses.

Top O' The Morning

Ingredients

3 small ripe bananas

3 cups unsweetened almond milk

1 1/2 teaspoons ground cinnamon

3 seedless oranges, peeled, cut in half

3 scoops protein powder

1 1/2 cups ice

Directions

1 Place all ingredients into the 40-ounce Master Prep Bowl in the order listed.

2 PULSE until smooth, using long pulses.

Tandoori Marinade
page 48

PREP TIME: **15** minutes   COOK TIME: **15** minutes   MAKES: **2 cups**
CONTAINER: **40-ounce Master Prep® Bowl**

Tandoori Marinade

Ingredients

2 ounces dried ancho chili peppers

$1/4$-inch piece fresh ginger, peeled

2 cloves garlic

$1/2$ cup fresh cilantro leaves

2 tablespoons garam masala powder

$1/8$ teaspoon ground nutmeg

1 tablespoon freshly squeezed lemon juice

1 cup nonfat Greek yogurt

$1/2$ cup cold water

Directions

1 Place the dried ancho chili peppers into a small saucepan and pour just enough water to cover the peppers. Bring to a boil, reduce to a simmer, and cook for 10 minutes. Strain peppers, discarding the liquid, and cool.

2 Remove the top and seeds from the peppers.

3 Place all ingredients into the 40-ounce Master Prep Bowl in the order listed. PULSE until desired consistency, using long pulses.

DO NOT BLEND HOT INGREDIENTS.

PREP TIME: **10 minutes**   MAKES: **2** cups
CONTAINER: **40-ounce Master Prep® Bowl**

Mango Rum Remoulade

Ingredients

1 1/2 cups light mayonnaise

1/3 cup cornichons

2 tablespoons drained capers

3 tablespoons dark rum

1 ripe mango, peeled,
pits removed, cut in 1-inch chunks

2 tablespoons water

1/2 teaspoon salt

Directions

1 Place all ingredients into the 40-ounce Master Prep Bowl in the order listed.

2 PULSE until desired consistency, using short pulses.

PREP TIME: **25 minutes**   COOK TIME: **30 minutes**   MAKES: **2 cups**
CONTAINER: **40-ounce Master Prep® Bowl**

Kale & Sunflower Seed Pesto

Ingredients

$1/2$ medium bunch kale, stems removed

$1/4$ cup fresh basil

1 large clove garlic

$1/4$ cup roasted unsalted sunflower seeds

2 tablespoons Parmesan cheese

Zest and juice of $1/2$ lemon

$1/4$ cup olive oil, plus more as needed

Salt, to taste

Ground black pepper, to taste

Directions

1 Bring 4 quarts salted water to a boil. Blanch kale leaves for 30 seconds and upon removal, immediately plunge into ice water. Squeeze kale leaves dry.

2 Add kale, basil, garlic, sunflower seeds, Parmesan cheese, lemon juice and zest, olive oil, and a pinch of salt and pepper to the 40-ounce Master Prep Bowl.

3 PULSE until desired pesto consistency is achieved. Add more oil if needed.

PREP TIME: **20 minutes**   COOK TIME: **40 minutes**   MAKES: **8–10 servings**
CONTAINER: **40-ounce Master Prep® Bowl**

Ratatouille Baked Ravioli

Ingredients

1 medium onion, peeled,
cut in quarters

1 small zucchini, cut in quarters

1 small yellow squash, cut in
quarters

1 small eggplant, cut in quarters

2 medium green bell peppers, cut
in quarters

8 plum tomatoes, cut in quarters

3 cloves garlic

$1/2$ teaspoon dried oregano

2 tablespoons olive oil

2 pounds frozen cheese ravioli,
cooked and drained

4 ounces fresh mozzarella cheese

Directions

1 Place onion into the 40-ounce Master Prep Bowl. PULSE until chopped (about 3 pulses). Transfer to a bowl.

2 Place zucchini, squash, eggplant, and green peppers into the 40-ounce Master Prep Bowl. PULSE until chopped (about 3 pulses). Transfer to a separate bowl.

3 Place tomatoes, garlic, and oregano into the 40-ounce Master Prep Bowl. PULSE until smooth, using long pulses. Transfer to a separate bowl.

4 Heat olive oil in a large skillet on medium-high heat. Add onions and cook until translucent, about 5 to 8 minutes. Add zucchini, squash, eggplant, and peppers, and sauté until they start to soften, about 10 to 15 minutes.

5 Add tomato mixture to skillet and simmer 5 to 10 minutes.

6 Place cooked ravioli into a 9x13-inch baking dish.

7 Pour vegetable tomato sauce over ravioli, making sure it is evenly distributed. Then spread sliced mozzarella over the top.

6 Bake uncovered, until golden, about 25 minutes.

DO NOT BLEND HOT INGREDIENTS.

PREP TIME: **15 minutes**   MAKES: **2 cups filling (4 pita sandwiches)**
CONTAINER: **40-ounce Master Prep® Bowl**

Mediterranean Tuna Pitas

Ingredients

$1/4$ cup red bell pepper, cut in 2-inch chunks, divided in half

$1/4$ cup green olives, pits removed, divided in half

$1/2$ small red onion, cut in 2-inch chunks, divided in half

1 stalk celery, cut in quarters, divided in half

1 solid white albacore tuna pouch (6.4 ounces) or 1 can (5 ounces)

$1/2$ cup plain Greek yogurt

1 tablespoon lemon juice

$1/2$ teaspoon dried oregano

2 round pitas

$1/4$ cup baby spinach

Directions

1 Place half the red pepper, olives, red onion, and celery into the 40-ounce Master Prep Bowl in the order listed.

2 Place half the tuna on top of the vegetables. Then place the remaining vegetables, followed by the remaining tuna, into the 40-ounce Master Prep Bowl.

3 PULSE until finely chopped, about 3 to 5 pulses. Scrape down sides of bowl if necessary during chopping. Transfer tuna salad to a mixing bowl; set aside.

4 To make the dressing, whisk together yogurt, oregano, and lemon juice. Add dressing to tuna salad.

5 To make the sandwiches, cut each pita in half, then divide the baby spinach and tuna salad between each of the 4 pita halves.

PREP TIME: **5 minutes**   CHILL TIME: **1 hour**   MAKES: **2 cups**
CONTAINER: *40-ounce Master Prep® Bowl*

Fresh Herb Ranch Dressing

Ingredients

1/2 cup light buttermilk

1 cup lowfat mayonnaise

1 tablespoon lemon juice

1/4 cup fresh parsley leaves

12 fresh chives, cut in half

2 tablespoons fresh tarragon leaves

1 clove garlic

1/2 teaspoon salt

1/8 teaspoon ground black pepper

Directions

1 Place all ingredients into the 40-ounce Master Prep Bowl in the order listed.

2 PULSE until smooth, using long pulses.

3 Chill dressing for at least 1 hour before serving to allow flavors to meld.

PREP TIME: **10 minutes**   COOK TIME: **10 minutes**   MAKES: **8 tacos**

CONTAINER: **40-ounce Master Prep® Bowl**

Taco Tuesday

Ingredients

1 pound uncooked boneless turkey breast, cut in 2-inch cubes

$1/2$ medium yellow onion, cut in quarters

1 tablespoon canola oil

1 package (1 ounce) low-sodium taco seasoning mix

8 hard taco shells

1 cup shredded lettuce

$1/2$ cup shredded lowfat cheddar cheese

$1/4$ cup jalapeño peppers

$1/3$ cup cilantro leaves

Best Blender Salsa, page 72

Directions

1 Place turkey and onion into the 40-ounce Master Prep Bowl. PULSE until finely ground, using short pulses.

2 Heat the oil in a medium skillet over medium heat and sauté turkey mixture for 6 to 8 minutes or until cooked. Add taco seasoning mix; stir to combine.

3 Assemble each taco with cooked turkey, lettuce, cheese, jalapeño peppers, cilantro, and our Best Blender Salsa.

PREP TIME: **20 minutes**   COOK TIME: **40 minutes**   MAKES: **8 servings**
CONTAINER: **40-ounce Master Prep® Bowl**

Vegetable Tortilla Soup

Ingredients

1 medium onion, cut in quarters

2 cloves garlic

1 medium jalapeño pepper

2 small zucchini, cut in quarters

1 jar (13 ounces) roasted
red peppers

4 plum tomatoes, cut in half

3 tablespoons olive oil

1/2 teaspoon ground coriander

1 teaspoon ground cumin

4 cups vegetable stock

1 cup frozen corn kernels, thawed

1/4 cup lime juice

Crushed tortilla chips, for garnish

Avocado slices, for garnish

Directions

1 Place onion, garlic, and jalapeño pepper into the 40-ounce Master Prep Bowl. PULSE until desired size (about 3 pulses). Transfer to a bowl; set aside.

2 Place zucchini into the 40-ounce Master Prep Bowl. PULSE until desired size (about 3 to 4 pulses). Transfer to a separate bowl; set aside.

3 Place roasted peppers into the 40-ounce Master Prep Bowl. PULSE until desired size (about 4 to 6 pulses). Transfer to a separate bowl; set aside.

4 Place tomatoes into the 40-ounce Master Prep Bowl. PULSE until desired size (about 4 to 6 pulses). Transfer to the bowl with the roasted peppers; set aside.

5 Add olive oil to a medium-sized soup pot over medium heat.

6 Add onion, garlic, and jalapeño pepper. Cook for 5 minutes, stirring frequently.

7 Add coriander and cumin and cook for 2 minutes.

8 Add roasted peppers and tomatoes. Cover and cook for 10 to 15 minutes, stirring occasionally.

9 Add vegetable stock and bring to a boil. Add zucchini, corn, and lime juice. Simmer uncovered for 15 minutes or until the zucchini becomes tender.

DO NOT BLEND HOT INGREDIENTS.

PREP TIME: 15 minutes   COOK TIME: 20-25 minutes   MAKES: 15 mini meatballs
CONTAINER: 40-ounce Master Prep® Bowl

Turkey Meatballs

Ingredients

1/2 pound uncooked dark turkey meat, cut in 1-inch cubes, well-chilled

1/4 onion, chopped

2 cloves garlic, peeled, minced

2 tablespoons fresh Italian parsley leaves, chopped

1/4 cup grated parmesan cheese

2 tablespoons breadcrumbs

1 tablespoon tomato paste

1 egg, beaten

Salt, to taste

Ground black pepper, to taste

Cooking spray

2 cups marinara sauce

Directions

1 Place the turkey into the 40-ounce Master Prep Bowl and PULSE to a fine chop. Do not overprocess.

2 Transfer the turkey to a bowl and add remaining ingredients, except cooking spray and marinara sauce. Mix to combine. Form mixture into 15 mini meatballs.

3 Lightly coat a large skillet with cooking spray. Over medium-high heat, sauté meatballs until browned on all sides, about 5 minutes. Add marinara sauce and simmer until sauce is thickened and meatballs are cooked through completely, about 15 to 20 minutes.

PREP TIME: 10 minutes   MAKES: 2 cups
CONTAINER: 40-ounce Master Prep® Bowl

Cilantro Mayonnaise

Ingredients

1 ½ cups cilantro leaves

1 ½ cups light mayonnaise

1 clove garlic

1 ½ teaspoons fresh lime juice

¼ teaspoon salt

Directions

1 Place all ingredients into the 40-ounce Master Prep Bowl in the order listed.

2 BLEND until smooth.

SERVE WITH A TURKEY BURGER, CHICKEN PANINI, OR EVEN BRUSHED ON A PIECE OF FISH.

PREP TIME: **15 minutes**   COOK TIME: **30 minutes**   MAKES: **4 servings**
CONTAINER: **40-ounce Master Prep® Bowl**

Broccoli Cheddar Soup

Ingredients

1/2 yellow onion, cut in half

1 clove garlic

1/2 tablespoon canola oil

3 cups broccoli florets

2 cups low-sodium vegetable broth

1/4 cup half & half

1/2 cup shredded cheddar cheese

Salt, to taste

Ground black pepper, to taste

Directions

1 Place the onion and garlic into the 40-ounce Master Prep Bowl. PULSE 3 to 5 times, using short pulses, until finely chopped.

2 Heat the oil in a medium saucepan over medium heat. Add the chopped onions and garlic and sauté for 5 minutes, until translucent.

3 Add the broccoli florets to the pot and cook 1 to 2 minutes. Add vegetable broth, bring to a boil and reduce heat to low and simmer 25 minutes until broccoli is fork tender. Add the half & half and the cheddar cheese then remove from heat. Cool to room temperature.

4 Working in batches, place half the cooled soup in the 40-ounce Master Prep Bowl and blend until smooth, using long pulses.

5 Place soup into a large bowl and repeat with remaining soup. Return puréed soup back to saucepan and simmer until heated through. Season with salt and pepper to taste.

DO NOT BLEND HOT INGREDIENTS.

PREP TIME: **20 minutes**   COOK TIME: **1 hour**   MAKES: **8 servings**
CONTAINER: **40-ounce Master Prep® Bowl**

White Bean & Chicken Chili

Ingredients

2 tablespoons olive oil

1 onion, chopped

1 green bell pepper, cored, chopped

3 cloves garlic, peeled, smashed

$3/4$ pound uncooked boneless, skinless chicken breasts, chilled

Salt, to taste

Ground black pepper, to taste

1 packet (1 ounce) chili seasoning

3 cans (15.5 ounces each) cannellini beans (2 cans drained)

2 cans (4 ounces each) diced green chiles

3 cups low-sodium chicken broth

1/2 cup shredded white cheddar cheese, for garnish

2 tablespoons chopped fresh cilantro leaves, for garnish

Directions

1 Heat the oil in a large soup pot over medium heat. Add the onion, green pepper, and garlic. Sauté until softened, stirring frequently.

2 Place chicken in the 40-ounce Master Prep Bowl. PULSE to a fine chop. Do not overprocess.

3 Add chicken, salt, pepper, and chili seasoning to the pot. Stir in 2 cans drained beans, green chiles, and chicken broth.

4 Place remaining can of beans with liquid in the 40-ounce Master Prep Bowl and PULSE until smooth. Add to chili and simmer for 30 to 40 minutes until slightly thickened.

5 Garnish each serving with shredded cheese and cilantro.

DO NOT BLEND HOT INGREDIENTS.

PREP TIME: **10 minutes**   MAKES: **2 servings**
CONTAINER: *40-ounce Master Prep® Bowl*

Savory Egg Salad

Ingredients

¹/₄ cup fresh parsley leaves

5 hard-boiled eggs, peeled

¹/₄ cup light mayonnaise

2 teaspoons Dijon mustard

¹/₈ teaspoon salt

¹/₄ teaspoon ground black pepper

¹/₄ teaspoon Worcestershire sauce

¹/₄ teaspoon onion powder

Directions

1 Place all ingredients into the 40-ounce Master Prep Bowl in the order listed.

2 PULSE until finely chopped, using short pulses.

 NINJA KNOW-HOW FOR A TASTY TWIST, TRY USING ¹/₄ CUP AVOCADO OR ¹/₄ CUP PLAIN GREEK YOGURT IN PLACE OF THE MAYONNAISE.

Sun-Dried Tomato Sauce

Ingredients

1 yellow onion, cut in quarters

4 cloves garlic

1 tablespoon olive oil

1 can (28 ounces) whole tomatoes and juice

$3/4$ cup sun-dried tomatoes packed in olive oil

$1/2$ cup dry red wine

$1/2$ teaspoon red pepper flakes

$1/2$ teaspoon salt

$1/8$ teaspoon ground black pepper

$1/4$ bunch fresh basil, chopped

Directions

1 Place the onion and garlic into the 40-ounce Master Prep Bowl and PULSE until roughly chopped, using short pulses.

2 In a medium saucepan over medium heat, heat the olive oil. Add the onions and garlic and sauté for 5 minutes, until softened.

3 Add the tomatoes with juice, sun-dried tomatoes, red wine, red pepper flakes, salt, and pepper to the 40-ounce Master Prep Bowl. PULSE, using short pulses, until desired consistency.

4 Add the tomato sauce to the saucepan with the garlic and onions. Simmer for 20 minutes. Add fresh basil at the end.

DO NOT BLEND HOT INGREDIENTS.

PREP TIME: **10 minutes**   MAKES: **4 servings**
CONTAINER: **40-ounce Master Prep® Bowl**

Tomato Basil Soup

Ingredients

1 can (28 ounces) crushed tomatoes

2 tablespoons tomato paste

1 clove garlic

1 cup vegetable broth

1/2 cup fresh basil

1/4 teaspoon salt

1/2 teaspoon ground black pepper

Directions

1 Place all ingredients into the 40-ounce Master Prep Bowl in the order listed.

2 PULSE until smooth, using long pulses.

3 Pour soup into a medium saucepan and simmer until heated through.

DO NOT BLEND HOT INGREDIENTS.

PREP TIME: **30 minutes + marinate 2 hours**   COOK TIME: **4 minutes**
MAKES: **4 servings**   CONTAINER: **40-ounce Master Prep® Bowl**

Tandoori Turkey Pita

Ingredients

1 pound uncooked turkey breast, cut in 2-inch cubes

¹⁄₄ cup Tandoori Marinade, page 40

4 (8-inch) whole wheat pita bread rounds

2 vine-ripe tomatoes, sliced

8 Boston lettuce leaves

¹⁄₃ cup Cucumber Feta Dip, page 79

Directions

1 In a medium bowl combine the cubed turkey and the Tandoori Marinade. Cover and chill for 2 hours.

2 Place the marinated turkey into the 40-ounce Master Prep Bowl and PULSE using short pulses, until finely ground.

3 Spray a nonstick skillet with vegetable cooking spray and place over medium heat. Add the ground turkey to the skillet and sauté, until cooked, about 4 minutes.

4 To assemble sandwich, cut pita bread rounds in half, open the pocket, place the lettuce and tomato in, and evenly divide the cucumber feta dip and cooked ground turkey into the pockets.

PREP TIME: **5 minutes**   MAKES: **2 servings**
CONTAINER: **40-ounce Master Prep® Bowl**

Curry Chicken Salad

Ingredients

$1/2$ pound cooked chicken breast, cut in 2-inch cubes

$1/4$ cup cilantro leaves

$1/4$ small red onion

1 celery stalk, cut in 3 pieces

$1/4$ cup light mayonnaise

2 teaspoons curry powder

2 teaspoons fresh lime juice

Directions

1 Place all ingredients into the 40-ounce Master Prep Bowl in the order listed.

2 PULSE until finely chopped, using short pulses.

Salmon Burgers

Ingredients

2 green onions,
cut in thirds

1 1/4 pound boneless and
skinless salmon, cut in
2-inch chunks

2 teaspoons Dijon mustard

1 tablespoon lemon juice

1 large egg

1/4 teaspoon Old Bay
seasoning

1/2 teaspoon ground
black pepper

1/4 cup panko breadcrumbs

Directions

1 Place all ingredients into the 40-ounce
Master Prep Bowl in the order listed.
PULSE, using short pulses, until desired
consistency. Form into 4 patties.

2 Spray a nonstick skillet or grill pan with
vegetable cooking spray and heat over
medium-high heat. Add burgers and
cook until golden brown on outside and
cooked through, about 3 minutes per
side. Serve on a whole wheat bun with
lettuce and tomato, or on a bed of your
favorite greens.

PREP TIME: **15** minutes   COOK TIME: **15** minutes   MAKES: **16** meatballs
CONTAINER: **40-ounce Master Prep® Bowl**

Asian Pork Meatballs

Ingredients

1 pound uncooked pork tenderloin, cut in 2-inch cubes

2 cloves garlic

$1/2$-inch piece fresh ginger, peeled

4 sliced green onions, divided

2 tablespoons low-sodium soy sauce

1 teaspoon ground coriander

1 large egg

Juice of 1 lime

$1/2$ cup fresh pineapple chunks

1 tablespoon whole-grain mustard

$1/2$ cup plain breadcrumbs

2 cups prepared sweet-and-sour sauce, warmed

Directions

1 Preheat oven to 350°F. Line a cookie sheet with parchment paper; set aside.

2 Place the pork, garlic, ginger, half of the green onions, soy sauce, coriander, egg, lime juice, pineapple, mustard, and breadcrumbs into the 40-ounce Master Prep Bowl and PULSE using long pulses, until finely ground.

3 Form into 16 meatballs and place on prepared cookie sheet. Bake for 15 minutes or until cooked through.

4 Toss meatballs with the warm sweet-and-sour sauce. Garnish with remaining green onions.

Spinach Artichoke Dip
page 74

PREP TIME: **5 minutes**   MAKES: **4 cups**
CONTAINER: **40-ounce Master Prep® Bowl**

Best Blender Salsa

Ingredients

1 can (14 ounces) whole peeled tomatoes

1 white onion, peeled, cut in quarters

¼ cup cilantro leaves

1 fresh jalapeño pepper, seeds removed

1 chipotle chile

2 tablespoons adobo sauce

1 lime, peeled, cut in quarters

Salt, to taste

Ground black pepper, to taste

Directions

1 Place all ingredients into the 40-ounce Master Prep Bowl in the order listed.

2 PULSE, to desired consistency, using short pulses, about 3 to 5 times.

 NINJA KNOW-HOW **FOR A TROPICAL VARIATION, ADD ½ CUP FRESH MANGO**

PREP TIME: 10 minutes   COOK TIME: 20 minutes   MAKES: 4 cups
CONTAINER: 40-ounce Master Prep® Bowl

Spinach Artichoke Dip

Ingredients

¹⁄₄ cup mayonnaise

¹⁄₄ cup sour cream

8 ounces cream cheese

2 tablespoons lemon juice

¹⁄₂ cup shredded lowfat
mozzarella cheese

¹⁄₂ cup grated Parmesan cheese

4 cloves garlic

1 can (14 ounces) artichoke hearts,
drained

1 cup frozen spinach, thawed,
excess liquid squeezed out

Directions

1 Preheat oven to 350°F. Place the mayonnaise, sour cream, cream cheese, lemon juice, mozzarella, Parmesan, and garlic into the 40-ounce Master Prep Bowl. PULSE 5 times, using long pulses.

2 Add the artichokes and spinach then PULSE 5 additional times, using short pulses, until mixed well.

3 Carefully remove the blades and spoon the dip into a heat-resistant baking dish. Bake for 20 minutes, until golden brown and bubbly. Serve warm with sliced French bread.

 NINJA KNOW-HOW   FOR A LIGHTER OPTION, USE LIGHT MAYONNAISE, LOWFAT CREAM CHEESE OR LOWFAT SOUR CREAM.

PREP TIME: 8 minutes   MAKES: 6 servings
CONTAINER: 40-ounce Master Prep® Bowl

Classic Bloody Mary

Ingredients

2 cans (8-ounces each) tomato sauce

1 lemon, peeled, cut in half, seeds removed

2 tablespoons prepared horseradish

2 teaspoons Worcestershire sauce

1 teaspoon hot sauce

1 teaspoon ground black pepper

$1/4$ teaspoons celery salt

$3/4$ cup vodka

4 cups ice

6 celery stalks, for garnish

Directions

1 Place all ingredients, except ice, into the 40-ounce Master Prep Bowl in the order listed.

2 PULSE until smooth, using long pulses. Divide Bloody Mary between 6 glasses of ice and garnish with a celery stalk.

PREP TIME: 5 minutes   MAKES: 2 $\frac{1}{2}$ cups
CONTAINER: 40-ounce Master Prep® Bowl

Classic Hummus

Ingredients

2 cups cooked, drained garbanzo beans (liquid reserved)

$\frac{1}{4}$ cup plus 2 tablespoons garbanzo bean liquid

$\frac{1}{4}$ cup lemon juice

$\frac{1}{4}$ cup olive oil

1 clove garlic

2 tablespoons tahini

1 teaspoon ground cumin

$\frac{1}{2}$ teaspoon salt

Directions

1 Place all ingredients into the 40-ounce Master Prep Bowl in the order listed.

2 PULSE until desired consistency, using long pulses.

PREP TIME: 15 minutes   COOK TIME: 15 minutes   MAKES: 1 cup filling (40 medium-sized stuffed mushrooms)
CONTAINER: 40-ounce Master Prep® Bowl

Baked Falafel Stuffed Mushrooms

Ingredients

1 can (15.5 ounces) garbanzo beans, drained

1/2 medium onion, cut in quarters

1/2 teaspoon garlic salt

1/2 teaspoon coriander

1/2 teaspoon ground cumin

1/4 teaspoon ground black pepper

2 tablespoons all-purpose flour

1 tablespoon lemon juice

1/2 teaspoon salt

1 tablespoon panko breadcrumbs

40 medium white mushroom caps

Directions

1 Preheat oven to 375°F.

2 Place all ingredients, except panko breadcrumbs and mushroom caps, into the 40-ounce Master Prep Bowl, in the order listed. PULSE to desired consistency, using long pulses. Scrape down sides of bowl as needed.

3 Rinse and dry mushrooms, then stuff them with the garbanzo bean mixture. Next, sprinkle panko breadcrumbs over them.

4 Bake for 15 minutes. Serve immediately.

PREP TIME: **10 minutes**   MAKES: **2 cups**
CONTAINER: **40-ounce Master Prep® Bowl**

Cucumber Feta Dip

Ingredients

¹/₄ small red onion

¹/₃ cucumber, cut in quarters

¹/₄ cup fresh dill

¹/₂ cup crumbled feta cheese

1 tablespoon freshly squeezed
lemon juice

¹/₂ teaspoon ground black pepper

Directions

1 Place all ingredients into the 40-ounce Master Prep Bowl in the order listed.

2 PULSE until desired consistency, using short pulses.

PREP TIME: 5 minutes   MAKES: 4 servings

CONTAINER: 40-ounce Master Prep® Bowl

Frozen Margarita

Ingredients

³/₄ cup tequila

¹/₄ cup triple sec

¹/₃ cup fresh lime juice

¹/₃ cup water

³/₄ cup frozen concentrated limeade

2 cups ice

Directions

1 Place all ingredients into the 40-ounce Master Prep Bowl in the order listed.

2 PULSE until smooth, using long pulses.

 KNOW-HOW SUBSTITUTE FROZEN STRAWBERRIES FOR THE ICE IN THIS RECIPE AND MAKE A DELICIOUS STRAWBERRY MARGARITA.

PREP TIME: **5 minutes**   MAKES: **4 servings**
CONTAINER: **40-ounce Master Prep® Bowl**

Banana Colada

Ingredients

1 ½ cups frozen pineapple chunks

1 ½ frozen ripe bananas

6 ounces light rum

1 ½ cups pineapple juice

³/₄ cup light coconut milk

³/₄ cup ice

Directions

1 Place all ingredients into the 40-ounce Master Prep Bowl in the order listed.

2 PULSE until smooth, using long pulses.

PREP TIME: **5 minutes**   MAKES: **6 servings**
CONTAINER: 40-ounce Master Prep® Bowl

Frozen Sangria

Ingredients

1 ¼ cups frozen strawberries

1 ¼ cups frozen pineapple chunks

1 ¼ cups frozen peach slices

1 lime, peeled, cut in half

1 seedless orange, peeled, cut in half

1 ¼ cups red wine

¼ cup brandy

Directions

1 Place all ingredients into the 40-ounce Master Prep Bowl in the order listed.

2 PULSE until smooth, using long pulses.

 FOR EXTRA FLAVOR, ADD ½ TEASPOON GROUND CINNAMON.

PREP TIME: **5 minutes**   MAKES: **4 servings**
CONTAINER: **40-ounce Master Prep® Bowl**

Piña Colada

Ingredients

2 ½ cups frozen pineapple chunks

2 cups ice

1 cup light coconut milk

²/₃ cup light rum

Directions

1 Place all ingredients into the 40-ounce Master Prep Bowl in the order listed.

2 PULSE until smooth, using long pulses.

PREP TIME: 5 minutes   MAKES: 2 servings
CONTAINER: 40-ounce Master Prep® Bowl

Frozen Mudslide

Ingredients

1 $^1/_4$ ounces vodka

1 $^3/_4$ ounces coffee liqueur

1 $^3/_4$ ounces Irish cream liqueur

2 $^3/_4$ cups ice

Whipped cream, for garnish

1 tablespoon chocolate syrup, for garnish

Directions

1 Place all ingredients, except whipped cream and chocolate syrup, into the 40-ounce Master Prep Bowl in the order listed.

2 PULSE until smooth, using long pulses.

3 Serve topped with whipped cream and a drizzle of chocolate syrup.

PREP TIME: **5 minutes**   MAKES: **3 servings**
CONTAINER: **40-ounce Master Prep® Bowl**

Walk on the Beach

Ingredients

$1/2$ cup vodka

$1/4$ cup peach schnapps

$1/2$ grapefruit, peeled, cut in quarters

$1/2$ lime, peeled

2 tablespoons grenadine

2 cups ice

Directions

1 Place all ingredients into the 40-ounce Master Prep Bowl in the order listed.

2 PULSE until smooth, using long pulses.

PREP TIME: 10 minutes   COOK TIME: 10 minutes   MAKES: 4 burgers
CONTAINER: 40-ounce Master Prep® Bowl

Weeknight Burger Bar

Ingredients

1 pound uncooked lean strip steak beef, cut in 1-inch cubes

Salt, to taste

Ground black pepper, to taste

1 tablespoon canola oil

4 whole wheat hamburger buns

4 lettuce leaves

4 slices tomato

4 slices lowfat cheddar cheese

Directions

1 Place the beef into the 40-ounce Master Prep Bowl.

2 PULSE to desired consistency, using short pulses.

3 Form into 4 patties; season with salt and pepper.

4 Heat the oil in a medium frypan over medium-high heat and sauté burgers for 4 minutes per side or to desired degree of doneness.

5 Serve on whole wheat buns with lettuce, tomato, and cheese, or on a bed of your favorite greens.

PREP TIME: 5 minutes   MAKES: 4 servings

CONTAINER: 40-ounce Master Prep® Bowl

Cool Watermelon Martini

Ingredients

2 cups fresh watermelon chunks

3 ounces vodka

2 ounces triple sec

2 tablespoons agave nectar

1 1/2 cups ice

Directions

1 Place all ingredients into the 40-ounce Master Prep Bowl in the order listed.

2 PULSE until smooth, using long pulses.

3 Serve in chilled martini glasses.

Peach Muffins
page 92

PREP TIME: 20 minutes   COOK TIME: 30 minutes   MAKES: 12 muffins
CONTAINER: 40-ounce Master Prep® Bowl

Peach Muffins

Ingredients

2 ripe peaches, pits removed, cut in quarters

1 teaspoon lemon juice

1/4 cup vegetable oil

1/2 cup lowfat milk

1/4 cup nonfat yogurt

2 teaspoons vanilla extract

1 large egg

3/4 cup sugar

1 3/4 cups all-purpose flour

2 teaspoons baking powder

1/4 cup ground flaxseed

1/2 teaspoon salt

Directions

1 Preheat oven to 350°F. Lightly coat a 12-cup nonstick muffin pan with cooking spray; set aside.

2 Place the peaches into the 40-ounce Master Prep Bowl and PULSE to finely chop, using short pulses. Remove peaches and set aside.

3 Place the lemon juice, oil, milk, yogurt, vanilla, and egg into the 40-ounce Master Prep Bowl and PULSE until smooth, using long pulses.

4 Add the sugar, flour, baking powder, flaxseed, and salt to the 40-ounce Master Prep Bowl and PULSE until combined, scraping bowl as needed. Do not overmix. Carefully remove blades and fold in the chopped peaches with a spatula.

5 Scoop the mixture into the prepared muffin pan, filling 3/4 full. Bake for 30 minutes or until a wooden toothpick inserted into the center comes out clean. Cool before serving.

PREP TIME: **10 minutes**   COOK TIME: **25 minutes**   MAKES: **12 servings**
CONTAINER: **40-ounce Master Prep® Bowl**

Carrot Cake

Ingredients

2 medium carrots, peeled, cut in 2-inch chunks

1 cup water

$1/2$ cup unsweetened applesauce

4 large eggs

1 (15.25 ounce) box carrot cake mix

Light Cream Cheese Frosting, page 101

Directions

1 Preheat oven to 325°F. Lightly spray the bottom of a 9x13-inch baking dish with vegetable cooking spray; set aside.

2 Place the carrots into the 40-ounce Master Prep Bowl and PULSE until chopped small, using short pulses.

3 Add remaining ingredients, except frosting, and PULSE, using short pulses, until ingredients are mixed well.

4 Pour batter into the prepared pan. Bake for 25 minutes or until a wooden toothpick inserted in the center comes out clean. Cool completely before frosting, if desired.

PREP TIME: **20 minutes**   COOK TIME: **40 minutes**   MAKES: **12 servings**
CONTAINER: **40-ounce Master Prep® Bowl**

Cheddar Jalapeño Corn Bread

Ingredients

1 cup lowfat milk

1/3 cup vegetable oil

1 large egg

1/3 cup sugar

1 teaspoon salt

1 cup yellow cornmeal

1 cup all-purpose flour

1 teaspoon baking soda

1 cup shredded cheddar cheese

2 fresh jalapeño peppers, seeds removed, chopped

1/2 cup canned corn, drained

Directions

1 Preheat oven to 350°F. Lightly coat a 9x9-inch baking dish with vegetable cooking spray; set aside.

2 Place the milk, oil, and egg into the 40-ounce Master Prep Bowl and PULSE 3 to 5 times, using long pulses.

3 Add the sugar, salt, cornmeal, flour, and baking soda and PULSE until combined, using long pulses, scraping bowl as needed. Do not overmix.

4 Carefully remove blades then fold in the cheese, jalapeño peppers, and corn. Pour the batter into the prepared baking dish.

5 Bake for 35 to 40 minutes or until a wooden toothpick inserted into the center comes out clean. Cool before serving.

PREP TIME: 5 minutes   MAKES: 4 servings

CONTAINER: 40-ounce Master Prep® Bowl

Raspberry Frozen Yogurt

Ingredients

1 ⅓ cups lowfat vanilla yogurt

1 tablespoon stevia

2 ½ cups frozen raspberries

Directions

1 Place all ingredients into the 40-ounce Master Prep Bowl in the order listed.

2 PULSE until smooth, using long pulses.

PREP TIME: **10 minutes**   COOK TIME: **25 minutes**   MAKES: **12 servings**
CONTAINER: **40-ounce Master Prep® Bowl**

Chocolate Espresso Cake

Ingredients

½ cup lowfat milk

½ cup coconut oil, melted

½ cup water

4 large eggs

2 tablespoons instant espresso

1 (3.9 ounce) package chocolate fudge pudding mix

1 (16.5 ounce) box dark chocolate fudge cake mix

Light Cream Cheese Frosting, page 101

Directions

1 Preheat oven to 350°F. Lightly spray the bottom of a 9x13-inch baking pan with vegetable cooking spray; set aside.

2 Place all ingredients, except frosting, into the 40-ounce Master Prep Bowl in the order listed and PULSE until smooth, using long pulses.

3 Pour batter into the prepared pan. Bake for 25 minutes or until a wooden toothpick inserted in the center comes out clean. Cool completely before frosting, if desired.

PREP TIME: **20 minutes**   COOK TIME: **35–40 minutes**   MAKES: **12 bars**
CONTAINER: **40-ounce Master Prep® Bowl**

Lemon Bars

Ingredients

1 cup (2 sticks) unsalted butter, softened

2 cups sugar, divided

2 $1/3$ cups all-purpose flour, divided

4 large eggs

$2/3$ cup freshly squeezed lemon juice

Confectioners' sugar, for dusting

Directions

1 Preheat oven to 350°F.

2 Place the butter, $1/2$ cup sugar, and 2 cups flour into the 40-ounce Master Prep Bowl. PULSE, using long pulses, until dough forms pea-sized crumbles. Press crust into the bottom of an ungreased 9x13-inch baking dish. Bake for 15 minutes or until firm and golden in color. Cool for 10 minutes.

3 Place the eggs, 1 $1/2$ cups sugar, $1/3$ cup flour, and lemon juice into the 40-ounce Master Prep Bowl. PULSE until smooth and sugar is dissolved, using long pulses. Pour mixture over the baked crust.

4 Bake 20 to 25 minutes. Bars will firm as they cool. Dust with confectioners' sugar when completely cooled.

PREP TIME: **20 minutes**   COOK TIME: **1 hour**   MAKES: **12 servings**
CONTAINER: **40-ounce Master Prep® Bowl**

Apple Bundt Cake

Ingredients

Vegetable cooking spray

4 green apples, peeled, cored, thinly sliced

2 large eggs

1 cup plus 4 teaspoons sugar, divided

1/2 cup vegetable oil

1/3 cup orange juice

2 teaspoons vanilla extract

2 cups all-purpose flour

1 teaspoon baking powder

1/4 teaspoon salt

2 teaspoons ground cinnamon

Directions

1 Preheat oven to 350˚F. Grease a Bundt pan with vegetable cooking spray; set aside.

2 Place sliced apples in a strainer.

3 Add eggs, 1 cup sugar, oil, orange juice, and vanilla extract to the 40-ounce Master Prep Bowl. PULSE until well mixed and sugar is dissolved.

4 Add flour, baking powder, and salt and PULSE until combined, scraping down sides of bowl as needed.

5 Drain liquid from apples.

6 Pour about 1/3 of the batter into the prepared pan, then add a layer of apples and dust with 1 teaspoon cinnamon and 2 teaspoons sugar. Repeat with batter and apples, ending with batter. Bake for approximately one hour or until a knife inserted in cake comes out clean.

7 Let cake cool for at least 1 hour before removing from pan.

PREP TIME: 5 minutes   MAKES: 1 1/2 cups
CONTAINER: 40-ounce Master Prep® Bowl

Cream Cheese Frosting

Ingredients

12 ounces lowfat cream cheese

3 tablespoons nonfat Greek yogurt

2 teaspoons vanilla extract

1 cup confectioners' sugar

Directions

1 Place all ingredients into the 40-ounce Master Prep Bowl in the order listed.

2 PULSE until smooth, using long pulses.

MAKE YOUR OWN FROSTING—ADD LEMON, LIME OR ORANGE ZEST. ADD A DROP OF YOUR FAVORITE EXTRACT, LIKE ALMOND OR PEPPERMINT TO CREATE DIFFERENT FLAVOR COMBINATIONS.

PREP TIME: **20 minutes**   MAKES: **1 crust**
CONTAINER: **40-ounce Master Prep® Bowl**

Basic Pie Dough

Ingredients

1 $1/4$ cups all-purpose flour

$1/2$ teaspoon salt

3 tablespoons cold unsalted butter, cut in half

3 tablespoons cold vegetable shortening stick, cut in half

$1/4$ cup cold water

Directions

1 Place the flour, salt, butter, and shortening into the 40-ounce Master Prep Bowl. PULSE, using long pulses, until pea-sized crumbles of dough form.

2 Add the water to the 40-ounce Master Prep Bowl and PULSE until dough just comes together. Do not overprocess.

3 Remove dough to a lightly floured work surface, gently form a ball, then flatten to a 1-inch disk. Wrap with plastic wrap and refrigerate until needed.

PREP TIME: 3 minutes   MAKES: 4 servings

CONTAINER: 40-ounce Master Prep® Bowl

Blueberry Sorbet

Ingredients

2 1/2 cups frozen blueberries

1 cup apricot nectar

Directions

1 Place all ingredients into the 40-ounce Master Prep Bowl in the order listed.

2 PULSE until smooth, using long pulses.

Chocolate Avocado Mousse

Ingredients

2 ripe bananas, cut in half

2 ripe avocados, cut in half, peeled, pits removed

1/4 cup chocolate sauce

Juice of 1/2 an orange

2 tablespoons cocoa powder

Directions

1 Place all ingredients into the 40-ounce Master Prep Bowl in the order listed.

2 PULSE until smooth, scraping down the sides of bowl as needed.

3 Place mousse into an airtight container and refrigerate until chilled.

SWEET TREATS

PREP TIME: 20 minutes   COOK TIME: 10–12 minutes   MAKES: 24 cookies
CONTAINER: 40-ounce Master Prep® Bowl

Gluten-Free Cherry Oaties

Ingredients

$^1/_2$ cup coconut oil

1 egg

$^1/_2$ teaspoon vanilla extract

$^1/_3$ cup packed brown sugar

$^1/_3$ cup granulated sugar

1 $^1/_4$ cups gluten-free flour

$^1/_2$ cup almond meal

$^1/_2$ cup gluten-free oats

$^1/_4$ cup unsweetened shredded coconut

$^1/_2$ teaspoon baking soda

1 teaspoon salt

$^1/_2$ teaspoon ground cinnamon

$^1/_2$ cup dried cherries, roughly chopped

Directions

1 Preheat oven to 350°F. Line 2 cookie sheets with parchment paper; set aside.

2 Place the coconut oil, egg, vanilla extract, brown sugar, and granulated sugar into the 40-ounce Master Prep Bowl. PULSE, using long pulses, until ingredients are combined. Scrape down sides of bowl as needed.

3 In a medium bowl, combine the flour, almond meal, oats, coconut, baking soda, salt, and cinnamon and stir to combine. Add half the dry mixture to the 40-ounce Master Prep Bowl. PULSE until combined, using long pulses. Scrape down sides of bowl, then add remaining dry mixture. PULSE until ingredients are mixed well.

4 Add the cherries to the 40-ounce Master Prep Bowl and PULSE 5 to 7 times, until cherries are evenly dispersed throughout dough.

5 Drop dough by rounded tablespoon onto prepared cookie sheets, about 2 inches apart. Bake for 10 to 12 minutes until just golden brown. Cookies will be very soft upon removal from oven but will set within 5 minutes of resting.

PREP TIME: 5 minutes   MAKES: 4 servings
CONTAINER: 40-ounce Master Prep® Bowl

Peach Ice Cream

Ingredients

2 ½ cups frozen peach slices

1 tablespoon fresh lime juice

3 tablespoons sugar

1 cup 2% reduced-fat milk

Directions

1 Place all ingredients into the 40-ounce Master Prep Bowl in the order listed.

2 PULSE until smooth, using long pulses.

 FEEL FREE TO USE YOUR FAVORITE MILK FOR THIS RECIPE, INCLUDING DAIRY-FREE OPTIONS LIKE ALMOND OR COCONUT MILK.

PREP TIME: 5 minutes   MAKES: 4 servings
CONTAINER: 40-ounce Master Prep® Bowl

Honey Nut Frozen Treat

Ingredients

2 cups sweetened oat milk

1 cup shelled walnuts

1/2 teaspoon vanilla extract

3 cups ice

3 tablespoons honey

Directions

1 Place all ingredients into the 40-ounce Master Prep Bowl in the order listed.

2 PULSE until smooth, using long pulses.

 IF YOU DON'T HAVE OAT MILK, ANY OTHER NON-DAIRY MILK CAN BE SUBSTITUTED.

Index

Notes